CRAZY
NATURE

Written by Sue Unstead
Design by Blue Sunflower Creative

First published by Parragon in 2009

Parragon
Queen Street House
4 Queen Street
Bath BA1 1HE, UK

ISBN 978-1-4075-7505-6

Printed in China

CRAZY NATURE

LIVE. LEARN. DISCOVER.

PaRragon

Bath · New York · Singapore · Hong Kong · Cologne · Delhi · Melbourne

WHAT'S ON THE PAGE

The pages of this book are packed with super stats and fantastic facts about our crazy planet. Here's what you'll find on the pages!

Introduction

Type of natural event

Fact File: Find out the crucial stats here.

DiscoveryFact™: Go to this section to find the most awesome fact on the page.

Watch out for bonus pages of quizzes and activities!

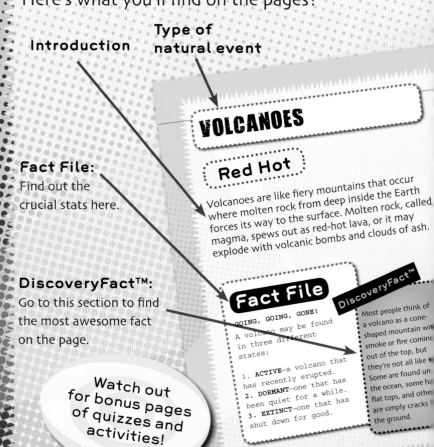

VOLCANOES

Red Hot

Volcanoes are like fiery mountains that occur where molten rock from deep inside the Earth forces its way to the surface. Molten rock, called magma, spews out as red-hot lava, or it may explode with volcanic bombs and clouds of ash.

Fact File

DiscoveryFact™

GOING, GOING, GONE!

A volcano may be found in three different states:

1. **ACTIVE**—a volcano that has recently erupted.
2. **DORMANT**—one that has been quiet for a while.
3. **EXTINCT**—one that has shut down for good.

Most people think of a volcano as a cone-shaped mountain wi smoke or fire comin out of the top, but they're not all like Some are found un the ocean, some ha flat tops, and othe are simply cracks the ground.

24

Visual key: Check out the key at the top right of each page for a quick guide to what type of natural event you're looking at.

Earthquake   Volcano   Water-related events

Storms

Fire-related events

Events directly relating to humans.

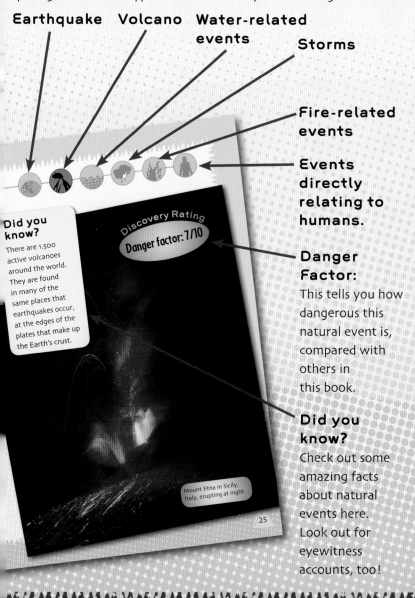

Discovery Rating

Danger factor: 7/10

Mount Etna in Sicily, Italy, erupting at night.

25

Danger Factor:
This tells you how dangerous this natural event is, compared with others in this book.

Did you know?
Check out some amazing facts about natural events here. Look out for eyewitness accounts, too!

RESTLESS EARTH

The Earth may feel solid under your feet but beneath the surface, molten rock is boiling and plates of rock are shifting and grinding together.

Beyond the land, the seas can build up giant waves, while lightning strikes and destructive winds can lash us from the sky.

In this book, you'll find out about the natural events that spring from the Earth, air, fire and water.

Earth

- volcanoes
- earthquakes

Air

- hurricanes
- tornadoes

Fire

- lightning strikes
- wildfires

Water

- tidal waves
- tsunamis
- floods

EARTHQUAKES

Making Shockwaves

The surface of the Earth is like a giant rocky jigsaw puzzle. The rocky plates—called tectonic plates—sit on a layer of hot molten rock and are constantly shifting about. When the plates grind against one another or collide, they create shock waves, which we feel as an earthquake.

Discovery Rating

Danger factor: 7/10

The damage in Castro, Chile, after an earthquake struck in 1960.

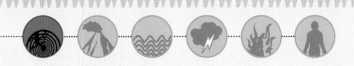

Fact File

THE WORLD'S WORST EARTHQUAKES...

MAGNITUDE	PLACE	YEAR
9.5	Chile, South America The largest ever recorded	1960
9.2	Alaska The largest in the U.S.	1964
9.1	Sumatra, Indonesia	2004
9.0	Kamchatka, Russia	1952
8.8	Ecuador, South America	1906
8.7	Aleutian Islands	1965
8.6	India/China border	1950
8.6	Aleutian Islands	1957
8.4	Morioka, Japan	1933

Did you know?

- Plates move at about the same speed as your fingernails grow.
- The epicenter is the spot on the Earth above the point where an earthquake occurs.

DiscoveryFact™

When a quake cracks open the ground, sulfur gases bubble up, smelling like rotten eggs.

THE RICHTER SCALE

Major or Minor

There are several ways to measure earthquakes. The strength, or "magnitude" of an earthquake can be measured by the Richter scale, which goes up in steps from 1. There is no top limit, but 7 or more is a major earthquake.

Fact File — EARTHQUAKE STATS...

* **Longest-lasting quake:** Alaska in 1964, which lasted 4 minutes. Few people were killed since it is such a deserted place.
* **Worst damage:** Kwanto, Japan, in 1923 at 8.3 on the Richter scale. The houses were built of wood and a firestorm destroyed the city and 575,000 homes.
* **Shock waves:** An earthquake can send shock waves traveling at 16,000 mph—more than 20 times the speed of sound. Shock waves can also spread out as far as 1,000 miles away.

Cover of "LIFE" magazine from 1964 after earthquake in Alaska.

Did you know?

Most quakes happen at the edges of the plates that make up the Earth's crust. A crack runs all around the rim of the Pacific Ocean. Over half of all earthquakes happen here.

scoveryFact™

As many as 500,000 earthquakes happen a year—that's about one a minute. But only about 1,000 cause severe damage.

SAN ANDREAS FAULT

San Francisco

Running the length of the west coast of the U.S. is the San Andreas Fault, a weak spot where two of the Earth's plates meet. In some places the plates are sliding past one another, in others they are pulling apart. As a result, earthquakes occur quite often along this invisible line.

Fact File

EARTHQUAKE CITY...

WHEN:	April 18, 1906	October 17, 1989
WHERE:	San Francisco	San Francisco
MAGNITUDE:	8.25	6.9
DURATION:	1 minute	15 seconds
DAMAGE:	25,000 buildings 250,000 homeless 450-700 killed $350 million	100,000 buildings 12,000 homeless 63 killed $6 billion

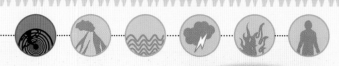

A house damaged by an earthquake in San Francisco.

DiscoveryFact™

Thousands of small earthquakes happen each year in California. The strongest 'quakes were in 1857, 1906, and 1989.

Eyewitness:

An eyewitness said, "The air was filled with falling stones. All around, the huge buildings were shaking and waving."

THE KOBE EARTHQUAKE

Danger Zone

In 1995, Japan was struck by the worst quake in 50 years. In spite of all its earthquake-proof buildings, more than one third of the people were left homeless. In places, the ground liquefied, turning into a thick soup so that buildings toppled over.

Fact File

KOBE FACTS...

WHEN:	5:46 a.m., January 17, 1995
WHERE:	Awajisma, 20 miles from Kobe, Japan
MAGNITUDE:	6.9
DURATION:	20 seconds
DAMAGE:	45,000 homes destroyed 6433 people killed $100 billion

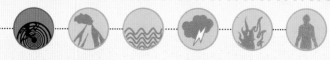

Discovery Rating

Danger factor: 8/10

Eyewitness:

A journalist reported: "The whole room was moving around like it was jelly."

As a result of the earthquake, a subway-train tunnel collapsed underneath this road in Kobe.

Did you know?

- Tokyo has the highest "at risk" rating from natural disasters of any of the world's big cities.
- A tremor occurs in Japan every five minutes.
- 2,000 tremors are felt by people each year.

SICHUAN PROVINCE

Early Warnings

Just before the 2008 quake in China, strange rainbow-colored cloud formations were seen in the sky. Scientists can't agree whether these were caused by gases released from the Earth or by electrical charges.

Discovery Rating

Danger factor: 9/10

A collapsed bridge in Sichuan, southwest China, in May 2008.

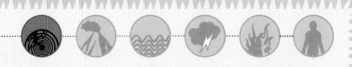

Did you know?

According to an ancient Japanese myth, earthquakes were caused by the thrashing tail of a giant catfish that lived deep under the Earth. There are many similar stories from different countries around the world.

DiscoveryFact™

Scientists who study the waves created by earthquakes are called seismologists. Seismometers are special machines that use electronic sensors to detect earthquakes and measure their strength.

Fact File

ANIMALS AND EARTHQUAKES...

* Some people believe animals can predict earthquakes.
* There are stories of dogs howling, cats going into hiding, fish jumping from the water, and birds taking flight just before a quake.
* Three days before a giant quake hit the city of Mianzhu, thousands of toads roamed the streets. Zebras in the zoo hit their heads against their cage door and elephants swung their trunks.
* Scientists put forward two possible theories:
  1. Animals sense vibrations in the Earth before humans can feel them.
  2. The movement of rocks causes electric signals that animals can sense.

EARTHQUAKE-PROOF BUILDINGS

Standing Strong

Some of the worst disasters in the past, such as the 1755 quake in Lisbon, Portugal, have been due to collapsing buildings. Studying the way that shock waves shake buildings has helped engineers and architects to build safe houses and even skyscrapers.

Fact File

TIP-TOP BUILDINGS...

* Pyramid or cone-shaped buildings are less likely to topple.
* Extra-strong concrete allows tall buildings to withstand shaking.
* The San Francisco International Airport building sits on giant ball bearings designed to allow the building to ride out a quake.
* The TransAmerica Building in San Francisco is cone-shaped and has special supports at the base that allow it to sway without collapsing.
* In Japan, traditional buildings like temple pagodas have a central steel column to help absorb shocks.

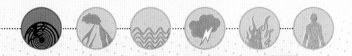

Did you know?

If buildings collapse, gas pipes may be broken. The slightest spark can cause a huge explosion. Fires break out that may be difficult to fight, because water pipes have been damaged.

The Transamerica Building in San Francisco.

DiscoveryFact™

Houses with wooden frames fare better than stone or brick buildings in a quake. Fastening a house onto its foundations helps, too.

SURVIVAL STORIES

Duck and Cover

People who live in earthquake zones have regular practices so they know what to do in an emergency.

Children are led through a practice earthquake drill at school.

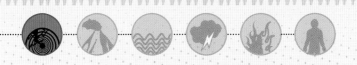

What to do if an earthquake strikes:

1. **Duck,** or drop down onto the floor
2. **Cover.** Take cover under a sturdy desk or table. Protect your head with your arms.
3. **Hold on** to your shelter and stay there until the shaking stops.

IRAN, 2004
A 97-year-old woman was rescued from rubble nine days after a major quake. Her bed was protected by an air pocket between two walls. When she was pulled out, she asked for a cup of tea. They knew she was a fighter when she grumbled that it was too hot to drink!

MEXICO, 1985
The huge quake that shook Mexico City destroyed many buildings. A family who lived on the first floor of a 14-story apartment building believed they were saved by their pet parrot. Rescuers heard the loud screeches of the bird from under the rubble of the collapsed building.

DiscoveryFact™

The safest place to stay during an earthquake is indoors, under a solid table or frame of an archway or doorway. Stay away from windows in case of breaking glass.

EARTHQUAKE QUIZ

1. The Earth's crust is made up of plates called:

a) dinner plates
b) fish plates
c) technical plates
d) tectonic plates

2. The point on the Earth above an earthquake is called:

a) the epicure
b) the epicenter

c) the target
d) the core

3. Sulfur gases smell like:

a) fish   c) rotten eggs
b) chocolate   d) your feet

4. The Earth's plates move at about the same speed as:

a) your hair grows   c) your skin grows
b) your fingernails grow   d) your nose grows

Answers on page 96!

5. Which major city has the biggest "at risk" rating from natural disasters?

a) Tokyo   c) London
b) Paris   d) New York

VOLCANOES

Red Hot

Volcanoes are like fiery mountains that occur where molten rock from deep inside the Earth forces its way to the surface. Molten rock, called magma, spews out as red-hot lava, or it may explode with volcanic bombs and clouds of ash.

Fact File

GOING, GOING, GONE!

A volcano may be found in three different states:

1. **ACTIVE**—a volcano that has recently erupted.
2. **DORMANT**—one that has been quiet for a while.
3. **EXTINCT**—one that has shut down for good.

DiscoveryFact™

Most people think of a volcano as a cone-shaped mountain with smoke or fire coming out of the top, but they're not all like this. Some are found under the ocean, some have flat tops, and others are simply cracks in the ground.

Did you know?

There are 1,500 active volcanoes around the world. They are found in many of the same places that earthquakes occur, at the edges of the plates that make up the Earth's crust.

Mount Etna in Sicily, Italy, erupting at night.

VOLCANO FACT FILE

Danger, danger!

When a volcano erupts, it's not just the eruption that causes damage. Rivers of red-hot lava flow down the volcano, clouds of ash and dust cover the area for months or even years, and landslides or mudflows of ash and water threaten nearby towns.

Lava flowing from erupting volcano on Reunion Island, Indian Ocean.

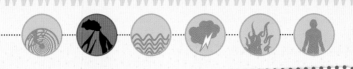

Fact File

THE BIGGEST EXPLOSIONS...

		ASH COLUMN HEIGHT (MILES)	VEI*	DEATHS
79	Vesuvius, Italy	18	5	2,000
186	Taupo, New Zealand	30	7	?
969	Baekdu, China	15	6-7	?
1452	Kuwae, South Pacific	4	?	?
1600	Huaynaputina, China	27	6	1,400
1815	Tambora, Indonesia	25	7	71,000
1883	Krakatoa, Indonesia	15	6	36,600
1902	Santa Maria, Guatemala	21	6	10,000
1912	Katmai, Alaska	20	6	2
1980	Mount St. Helens	12	5	57
1985	Mount Ruiz, Colombia	16	3	23,000
1991	Pinatubo, Philippines	21	6	1,202

* VEI means Volcanic Explosion Indicator and measures the explosiveness of a volcanic eruption.

Did you know?

The largest active volcano is Mauna Loa, in Hawaii, with a diameter of 62 miles. The highest active volcano is Llullaillaco, in Chile, measuring 22,057 feet high.

DiscoveryFact™

The world's most active volcano is in Kilauea, Hawaii. It has erupted non-stop since 1983!

MOUNT ST. HELENS

Eruption!

This snow-capped mountain on the west coast of the U.S. had been quiet for over 100 years. Early in 1980, a series of earthquakes and a plume of steam showed it was coming to life...

Fact File

MOUNT ST. HELENS STATS...

WHEN:	8:32 a.m., May 18, 1980
WHERE:	Mount St. Helens, Washington state
VEI:	5
ASH COLUMN:	12 miles into air
DAMAGE:	250 square miles land devastated
	57 deaths
	$1.1 billion

* Landslides buried the mountain under huge mounds of debris.
* Most trees were flattened by the blast.
* Water from melting ice mixed with debris and ash, forming mudflows.

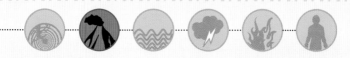

Eyewitness:

A photographer reported, "The sight was so overwhelming that I became dizzy and had to turn away to keep my balance."

Did you know?

The initial explosion continued for nine hours. The eruption cloud spread across the U.S. in three days and around the Earth in 15 days.

Big clouds of steam and ash erupting from Mount St. Helens.

29

KRAKATOA

Big Bang

Discovery Rating

Danger factor: 10/10

The biggest bang ever heard on the Earth happened in 1883 when Krakatoa exploded with a power 67,000 times greater than the atomic bomb dropped on Japan in World War II. Two-thirds of the island was thrown 50 miles into the air.

Did you know?

Dust from Krakatoa traveled around the world in the atmosphere, causing dramatic sunsets and turning the moon blue.

Krakatoa erupting with a column of ash.

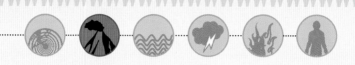

Fact File

CRACKING KRAKATOA...

WHEN:	10:02 a.m., August 27, 1883
WHERE:	Krakatoa, Indonesia
VEI:	6
ASH COLUMN:	15 miles
DAMAGE:	9 square miles of island disappeared 36,000 deaths

* The eruption destroyed the island. Darkness fell as a huge cloud of ash and dust blotted out the sun.
* The explosion caused a huge wave of water, or tsunami, that spread out as far as California and South Africa. More than 100 feet tall, it smashed everything in its path. Ships were carried 1 mile inland.

DiscoveryFact™

People heard the blast of Krakatoa 2,400 miles away in Australia. The earthquake was felt 9,000 miles away in California.

MOUNT VESUVIUS

Roman Tale of Terror

Clouds of ash and dust rained down on the people of Pompeii in Italy when Mount Vesuvius erupted in A.D. 79. The people choked to death or were burned alive. The nearby town of Herculaneum was engulfed in debris.

Fact File
STATS ON VESUVIUS...

WHEN:	10:00 a.m., August 24, A.D. 79
WHERE:	Vesuvius, Italy
VEI:	5
ASH COLUMN:	18.5 miles
DURATION:	24 hours
DAMAGE:	Towns of Pompeii and Herculaneum Over 2,000 deaths
ERUPTIONS:	1631, 1767, 1779, 1885, 1906, 1944

✳ Herculaneum was hit by hot ash and pumice, which buried it to a depth of 65 feet.

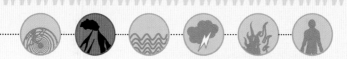

Eyewitness:

The historian Pliny wrote, "It was now day everywhere else, but here a deeper darkness prevailed than in the thickest night."

Discovery Rating

Danger factor: 10/10

Did you know?

The pumice and ash preserved Pompeii in a layer of dust. Archaeologists are able to make perfect casts of Pompeii's victims by pouring plaster into the hollows left when soft body parts decayed.

The giant crater at the top of Mount Vesuvius, Naples, Italy.

TAMBORA

Greatest Volcanic Eruption

The volcano that beats all the records is Tambora in Indonesia, producing over 19 cubic miles of ash when it erupted in 1815. The force of the eruption had four times the energy of Krakatoa and 100 times that of Mount St. Helens.

Fact File   TROUBLE AT TAMBORA...

WHEN:	April 10-11, 1815
WHERE:	Tambora in Sumbawa, Indonesia
VEI:	7
ASH COLUMN:	27 miles

DAMAGE: Ash layer 0.3 inches thick fell on 193,000 square miles of Indonesia and the Java Sea.
35,000 homes were destroyed.
50,000 islanders died and more were killed by famine and disease.

STILL ACTIVE?	Yes

* The explosion was heard 1,600 miles away.
* Lava flowed 12.5 miles from the summit.
* The eruption blew away one third of the mountain's cone.

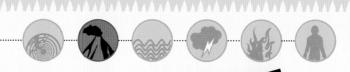

Discovery Rating

Danger factor: 7/10

DiscoveryFact™

The most explosive volcano of the 20th century was Mount Pinatubo in the Philippines in 1991.

An ash shower in the Philippines, following the eruption of Volcano Pinatubo in January 2008.

Did you know?

1816, the year following Tambora's eruption, was known as a year "without a summer" in Europe and North America. Ash darkened the skies for months.

MOUNT RUIZ

Deadly Landslide

In 1985, a fairly small eruption happened in the Andes Mountains. The ice cap on Mount Ruiz was melted by hot lava flows, sending a sudden surge of meltwater and ash in huge flows down the volcano's slopes. The town of Armero 3 miles below was completely buried.

Fact File

THE SLEEPING LION...

WHEN:	9:30 p.m., November 13, 1985
WHERE:	Mount Ruiz, Colombia, South America
VEI:	3
ASH COLUMN:	17 miles
DAMAGE:	Armero town buried in mud 23,000 deaths

* Locals called the mountain "The Sleeping Lion."
* The tragedy was that scientists knew the volcano would erupt but the town was not evacuated.

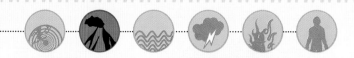

DiscoveryFact™

From the time of eruption, it took 15 minutes for the mud flow to reach the town. It was traveling at 30 mph. More waves came and the mud then solidified. Only one in ten of the inhabitants survived.

Eyewitness:

A boy who escaped to higher ground with his brother said, "The mud was coming behind us. We had run two blocks, but by the third block we were surrounded."

Armero in Colombia, flooded after the eruption of Mount Ruiz.

SURVIVAL STORIES

Please Stand Back

Volcanoes are unpredictable but not as dangerous as earthquakes or hurricanes. The best way of keeping safe is to stay as far away as possible.

Did you know?

Around 500 million people around the world live in a volcano zone.

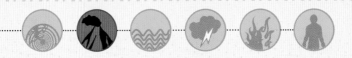

Fact File

Your chance of being killed by a volcano is quite slim compared with these other risks.

CHANCE OF DYING IN AN ACCIDENT:

Car accident	1 in 80
Taking a bath	1 in 10,000
Storm	1 in 17,000
Bee sting	1 in 76,000
Volcano eruption	1 in 80,000

DiscoveryFact™

John Slemp had a very lucky escape when he fell 2,000 feet into the crater of Mount St. Helens. He slipped and landed on a snow bank. It collapsed and he fell another 1,500 feet. Rescuers were amazed when he was pulled out unharmed!

Volcanologists explore a volcano in Italy, surrounded by ash and gases.

VOLCANO TRUE OR FALSE?

Are these volcano facts true or false?

1.
There are 150 active volcanoes around the world.

2.
Molten rock is called magma.

3.
Volcanoes may be found under the ocean.

4.
The world's most active volcano is Mauna Loa in Hawaii.

5.
When Mount Krakatoa erupted in 1883 it was the biggest bang ever heard on the Earth.

6.

Mount Vesuvius in Italy has only erupted once.

7.

You are more likely to be killed by a volcano than in a car accident.

8.

VEI stands for Volcanic Explosion Indicator.

9.

The mudslide that struck the town of Armero, Peru in 1985 was traveling at 300 mph.

10.

The best way of keeping safe from a volcano is to wear a hat.

Answers on page 96!

TSUNAMI

Making Waves

A tsunami (pronounced "soo–naam–ee") is a giant sea wave, thrown up by underwater earthquakes and sometimes by volcanic eruptions. Tsunamis are different from ordinary waves.

Fact File

ALL ACROSS THE SEA...

On May 21-22, 1960, two earthquakes occurred off the coast of Chile.

15 MINUTES LATER: A 33-foot-high tsunami hit the coast, killing 2,300 people.

15 HOURS LATER: A 36-foot-high tsunami flooded Hawaii, killing 61 people.

22 HOURS LATER: A 20-foot-high wave hit Japan, killing 122 people.

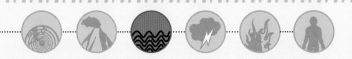

Did you know?

A tsunami spreads out like ripples in a pond. In the deep ocean they may be only 3 feet high, but they build up into a wall of water 100-130 feet high when they reach land. Ships are tossed inland, houses crushed, trees and all vegetation swept away, and inland areas flooded.

DiscoveryFact™

80% of all tsunamis occur in the Pacific. That's because in the "Ring of Fire" all around the ocean there are many earthquakes and volcanoes.

Large waves breaking on the coast of Tahiti in the South Pacific.

TSUNAMI FACT FILE

Major Tsunamis

The highest tsunami recorded was in Alaska in 1958, measuring 1,700 feet. That's almost twice the height of the Eiffel Tower!

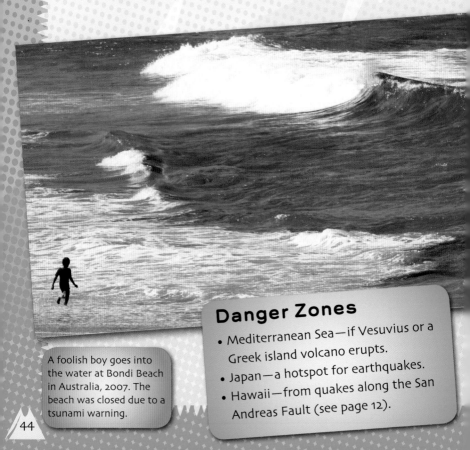

A foolish boy goes into the water at Bondi Beach in Australia, 2007. The beach was closed due to a tsunami warning.

Danger Zones

- Mediterranean Sea—if Vesuvius or a Greek island volcano erupts.
- Japan—a hotspot for earthquakes.
- Hawaii—from quakes along the San Andreas Fault (see page 12).

The earliest recorded tsunami was in 426 B.C. The Greek historian Thucydides wrote: "The sea returned in a huge wave and invaded a great part of the town."

Did you know?

If Cumbre Vieja volcano in the Canary Island of La Palma erupts, tsunamis could travel right across the Atlantic to destroy cities like New York, Boston, Washington, and Miami.

Fact File

MAJOR TSUNAMIS...

DATE	PLACE	CAUSE	DEATHS
c.1410 B.C.	Santorini	volcano	100,000
1498 A.D.	Nankaido, Japan	earthquake	31,200
1707	Todaido, Japan	earthquake	30,000
1755	Lisbon, Portugal	earthquake	100,000
1782	South China Sea	earthquake	40,000
1868	North Chile	earthquake	25,674
1883	Krakatoa	volcano	36,500
1896	San Riku	earthquake	26,360
1964	Alaska	earthquake	119
1998	Papua New Guinea	earthquake	2,182

SUMATRA

A Giant Wave

One of the largest-ever tsunamis swamped the coasts of 12 countries, including Indonesia, Sri Lanka, and Thailand on December 26, 2004.

Discovery Rating

Danger factor: 9/10

A building ruined by the tsunami in Banda Aceh.

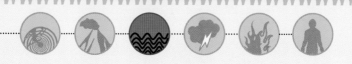

Did you know?

The sea was sucked out first, revealing flapping fish and old shipwrecks, before the huge wall of water approached.

Fact File

WHEN:	December 26, 2004
WHERE:	Formed off coast of Sumatra. Hit Banda Aceh first
CAUSE:	Underwater earthquake measured 9 on Richter scale
HEIGHT OF WAVE:	33 feet
DAMAGE:	$13 billion rebuilding costs 300,000 people dead Over 5 million homeless

* The land was scattered with wreckage and stripped of all trees and greenery.
* The sea flooded vast areas inland.
* Aid agencies worked together to provide help from all around the world.

DiscoveryFact™

The effects were felt as far away as Antarctica and South America.

SURVIVOR STORIES

Disappearing Water

In 2004, an English girl was on vacation with her family on Phuket Island, Thailand. When she saw the water disappearing, she remembered her geography lessons and knew that a wave was about to happen. She shouted at people to run and saved many lives.

A new tsunami warning buoy near Phuket Island, being checked by an official.

Fact File

SURVIVAL TIPS...

What to do if a tsunami threatens:

* Get as far away from the water as possible.
* Climb to a high hill or even up a tree.
* Remember that there will be more than one wave and that the second may be bigger than the first.

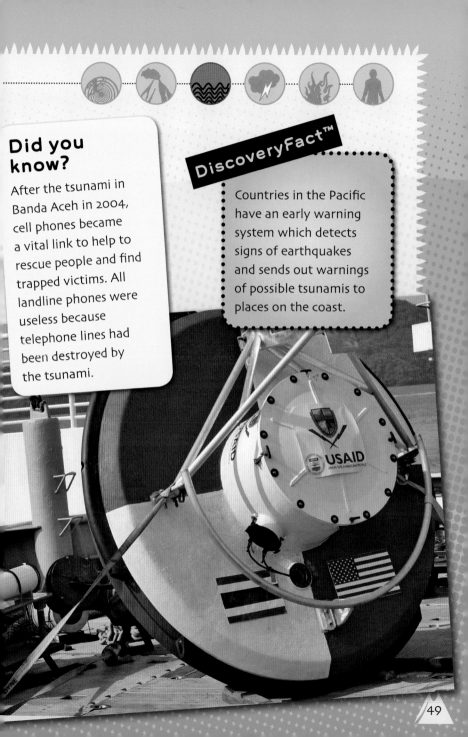

After the tsunami in Banda Aceh in 2004, cell phones became a vital link to help to rescue people and find trapped victims. All landline phones were useless because telephone lines had been destroyed by the tsunami.

DiscoveryFact™

Countries in the Pacific have an early warning system which detects signs of earthquakes and sends out warnings of possible tsunamis to places on the coast.

USAID
FROM THE AMERICAN PEOPLE

HURRICANES

Terrible Storms

These powerful tropical storms are the most destructive of all natural disasters. Hurricanes form when bands of thunderstorms pick up moist air from warm seas near the Equator. The spin of the Earth sets the storms rotating and a hurricane is born.

The eye of a hurricane, viewed by satellite.

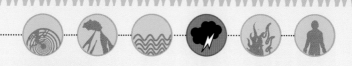

In the hurricane-prone Caribbean, there is a myth that an evil god called Hurican is the cause of the strong winds. In Taiwan, the wind god Hung Kong is a giant bird that flaps its wings, causing storms over the South China Sea.

Did you know?

In the U.S. the official hurricane season is June 1 to November 30. That's when a hurricane is most likely to hit, although they can happen any time of year.

Fact File

FACTS ABOUT HURRICANES...

* Hurricanes form over the ocean in warm tropical waters.
* They can be up to 10 miles high and 1,000 miles wide.
* A storm becomes a hurricane when winds reach 75 mph.
* In the center of a hurricane is a calm area called the eye.
* The strongest winds are in the wall of the eye.
* The real damage happens when hurricanes hit the land.
* The Saffir-Simpson scale is used to measure the force of the wind and the damage it causes. The scale ranges from category 1 (75-95 mph) to category 5 (155 mph and over).

HURRICANES A-Z

Storm Alphabet

Since 1972, hurricanes in the Atlantic have been given names to identify them, working through a list of boys' and girls' names each year.

Eyewitness:

An eyewitness to a hurricane in Galveston, Texas, in 1900 said, "About 3,000 homes had been completely swept out of existence. Where 20,000 people lived on the 8th, not a house remained on the 9th."

DiscoveryFact™

Most names for hurricanes are used several times. However, if a hurricane is particularly deadly or destructive, the name it was given is "retired" and never used again.

Fact File

GALVESTON, TEXAS, 1900
WINDS: 130 mph
DAMAGE: $68 million
8,000 people died, many from watching the storm surge of the sea.

THE GREAT MIAMI HURRICANE, 1926
WINDS: 150 mph
DAMAGE: $100 million
Over 300 people dead.

THE LABOR DAY HURRICANE, FLORIDA, 1935
WINDS: 185 mph
DAMAGE: $6 million
400-600 people dead.

HURRICANE CAMILLE, FLORIDA, 1969
WINDS: 190 mph
DAMAGE: $1.42 billion
259 people dead.

HURRICANE ANDREW, FLORIDA, 1992
WINDS: 102 mph
DAMAGE: $26.5 billion
Many people homeless.
43 people dead.

HURRICANE MITCH, FLORIDA, 1998
WINDS: 180 mph
DAMAGE: $3 billion damage
3 million people homeless.
11,000 people dead, due to flooding.

View of Hurricane Andrew over Florida in 1992.

HURRICANE KATRINA

New Orleans Nightmare

Hurricane Katrina was the most costly and destructive storm in U.S. history. It began in the Bahamas, developed into a hurricane and moved across the top of Florida, into the Gulf of Mexico. The city of New Orleans was in its path. A huge storm surge flooded the entire city as water broke through the banks.

Fact File
KATRINA STATS...

WHEN:	August 29, 2005
WHERE:	Gulf Coast, U.S. (landfall in New Orleans)
HIGHEST WINDS:	175 mph
STORM SURGE:	29 feet
DAMAGE:	$81 billion
	1,800 people dead. 80% of New Orleans flooded.

DiscoveryFact™

The Louisiana Superdome stadium became an official hurricane center.

New Orleans in
September 2005,
after Hurricane
Katrina struck.

Did you know?

- People had been advised to leave the city, but poorer people with no cars were stranded when buses and trains stopped.
- Many people were trapped by the rising floodwaters, an evil-smelling soup of diesel, dead animals, debris, mud, and sewage.
- Chaos descended with looters and gangs.
- The authorities were criticized for not getting help quickly to where it was needed.

TYPHOONS AND CYCLONES

Tropical Storms

In the Indian Ocean, tropical storms are called cyclones, while in the northwest Pacific they are called typhoons. South of the Equator storms spin counterclockwise, while north of the Equator they spin clockwise. This is caused by the motion of the Earth.

Discovery Rating
Danger factor: 8/10

A flooded street in Manila during the heavy rain of typhoon Sinlaku in September 2008.

BANGLADESH CYCLONE, 1991

WINDS: 160 mph

DAMAGE: 140,000 deaths
10 million people affected.
790,000 homes destroyed.

TYPHOON BILIS, TAIWAN, 2000

WINDS: 200 mph

DAMAGE: 11 people dead.

CYCLONE ZOE, SOLOMON ISLANDS, 2002

WINDS: 230 mph

DAMAGE: One of the most intense storms, but no one killed.

CYCLONE NARGIS, BURMA, 2008

WINDS: 135 mph

DAMAGE: 138,000 people dead.
2.4 million people affected.
11.5-foot storm surge caused terrible floods.

DiscoveryFact™

The highest storm surge caused by winds occurred when tropical cyclone Mahina struck Bathurst Bay, Australia, with a 43-foot sea surge. Fish and dolphins were found on top of cliffs.

Did you know?

The highest rainfall caused by a storm fell in 1966 during tropical storm Denise, La Reunion. 45 inches of rain fell in 12 hours.

OUT AT SEA

The Perfect Storm

Ships out on the ocean try to avoid the path of a hurricane at all costs. Going into port is not an option since the sea will be even rougher near the coast. It is better to close all the hatches and ride out the storm, running downwind.

Fact File

THE STORMIEST SEAS...

- 1995: A wave 94 feet high struck an oil rig on the North Sea.
- 1996: Italian cruise ship Michaelangelo en route to New York had a hole torn in its superstructure 80 feet above the waterline. A crew member and 2 passengers were killed.
- 1996: British cruise ship Queen Elizabeth II recorded a freak wave 96 feet high. The captain reported that it "came out of darkness like the white cliffs of Dover."
- 2005: 4 passengers were injured on the Norwegian Dam when a 7-story wave smashed windows at the level of the 10th deck.

Did you know?
Sometimes ships leave harbor to avoid storm surges and buffeting in harbor.

A fishing trawler at sea during a storm on the North Sea.

DiscoveryFact™

Thirteen ships were in the harbor of Apia, Samoa, in 1889, when a hurricane was forecast—six U.S. ships, six German ships and the British ship "Calliope." By dawn, ships were dragging anchors and being driven on to the reef. Bravely, "Calliope" headed out to sea, battling wind and waves. Two days later, she returned to find that all the other ships had been wrecked.

LANDFALL

Swirling Winds

Once a hurricane hits the coast, it slows down, but the swirling winds are still strong enough to cause terrible destruction.

Discovery Rating

Danger factor: 8/10

Houses sit among debris after Hurricane Ike hit Crystal Beach, Texas in September 2008.

DiscoveryFact™

- Storm shutters keep out the winds and protect the glass.
- Special ties and bolts prevent roofs and doors from being blown off.
- A strong metal "safe room" or cellar provides shelter.
- Sandbags keep out water or rain.

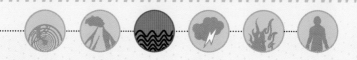

Fact File

HURRICANE WARNINGS...

In the U.S. and many other countries, flags are flown to warn of a storm on its way.

- **HURRICANE ALERT**: A red flag means a hurricane is 72 hours away.
- **HURRICANE WATCH**: A red flag with a black spot means a hurricane is 36 hours away.
- **HURRICANE WARNING**: Two red flags with black spots mean a hurricane is 24 hours away.
- **ALL CLEAR**: A green flag means the coast is clear.

People living in hurricane zones are told to be ready for the hurricane season by:
1. Following instructions if you are told to leave the area.
2. Going somewhere away from the coast or staying with a relative.
3. Taking an emergency kit containing water, food, spare clothing, first aid kit, flashlight, and battery-powered radio.

Did you know?

In areas where hurricanes are common, specially built hurricane shelters can give protection. Often built on stilts to cope with any flooding, they are designed to withstand high winds.

TROPICAL STORM QUIZ

1. What is the central part of a hurricane called?

   a) The hub
   b) The heart
   c) The eye
   d) The vortex

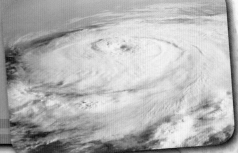

2. Which way do tropical storms spin when they are north of the Equator?

   a) North to south
   b) Clockwise
   c) In loops
   d) Counterclockwise

3. Where might you find a cyclone?

a) In the Atlantic
b) In the Pacific
c) In the Mediterranean
d) In the Indian Ocean

4. Which part of a hurricane is the most windy?

a) The eye
b) The wall

5. Which hurricane flooded the city of New Orleans?

a) Katrina
b) Kevin
c) Kathleen
d) Karen

Answers on page 96!

TORNADOES

In a Spin

A hurricane loses its energy when it hits land, but it can also generate another kind of deadly storm, called a tornado. Tornadoes are vertical funnels of rapidly spinning air. These wild and destructive storms are born in giant thunderstorms.

Fact File

TORNADO TROUBLE...

* Tornadoes can cut a path 1 mile wide and 50 miles long.
* Winds can reach 250 mph.
* Funnels can be up to 650 feet wide.
* Tornadoes move at 10-20 mph but some have reached 70 mph.
* Average warning time is 13 minutes. Watch out for a dark greenish sky, large hailstones, and a roaring sound.

Dark storm clouds about to form a tornado.

DiscoveryFact™

Tornado Alley is a major hotspot, running from South Dakota through Kansas and Oklahoma. An average of 1,000 tornadoes form here a year.

Did you know?

Great Britain holds the record for the highest number of tornadoes (60) per 0.5 miles. Surprised? Yes, but it's a much smaller country than the U.S.

SKY SHOWERS

Raining Fish and Frogs!

Really surprising things fall out of the sky after a tornado has passed by. The swirling funnel of wind can pick up all kinds of objects.

Fact File

FLYING ANIMALS...

* **TOADS:** In June, 1997, a village in Mexico had a shower of toads that rained down from the sky.
* **FROGS:** In 1998 in Croydon, England, it rained frogs instead of rain.
* **BABIES:** In Messina, Italy, a sleeping baby was plucked from its carriage and safely put down on a grassy slope nearby.
* **COKE CANS:** In 1995 in Iowa, a shower of cans fell from the sky, having traveled from a bottling plant 100 miles to the north.
* **FRESH FISH:** A shower of sprats fell onto surprised shoppers in Great Yarmouth, England, in 2000.

Discovery Rating

Danger factor: 5/10

Did you know?

Tornadoes are classified as weak, strong, or violent. Only 2 percent of tornadoes are classified as violent. Most deaths are caused by flying debris.

DiscoveryFact™

The Bible is full of references to plagues of frogs, flies and locusts. Perhaps they were caused by tornadoes...

A tornado carries flying debris in Texas, 1995.

STORM CHASERS

Hurricane Hunters

Most of us would run in the opposite direction at the news of wild weather approaching, but some people actually go out looking for storms. Hurricane hunters try to get into the fiercest winds to measure windspeeds.

Fact File

STORM DATA...

* The aircraft commonly known as "Snoopy" for its nose cone covered in instruments, flies with storms to measure windspeed and turbulence. Data is sent to weather stations to help track the directions of storms.

* Special instruments using doppler radar can detect the speed and direction of storms and predict the formation of tornadoes.

DiscoveryFact™

The U.S. Force Reserve 53rd Weather Reconnaissance Squadron flies right into the eye of a storm to predict the exact landfall so that people can be evacuated and take action.

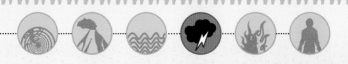

Discovery Rating
Danger factor: 5/10

Did you know?
Storm chasers drop instruments protected in a strong metal casing right in the path of a storm to measure windspeeds... and then run like mad!

The instruments on this storm-chaser's car can read the atmosphere's temperature, humidity, wind speed, and direction.

DUST DEVILS

Wicked Whirlwinds

Over deserts or in places where the ground is heated up by a fierce sun, dust devils can form. Sand is sucked up to create a whirlwind.

Discovery Rating
Danger factor: 5/10

Fact File

DUST DEVIL INFO...

* Dust devils can reach nearly 5,000 feet high.
* They can be up to 1.25 miles wide.
* Dust devils are short-lived but as one dies down, another rises up.
* They are known as "sand pillars" when they travel across deserts.
* Australians call these dust devils "willy willy" or "whirly whirly."
* In Egypt, the storms are known as "ghost's wind."
* In Brazil, these storms are called "redemoinho" after the name for a windmill.

Navajo Indians in North America believed dust devils were caused by chindii—spirits of dead Navajos. If they spun clockwise, they were good spirits; if counterclockwise, they were bad spirits.

Did you know?

Dust devils occur on the planet Mars. They were first photographed by orbiters sent there by NASA. One result was that dusty solar panels were scoured clean by a dust devil. After that it worked much better!

A dust devil in the Atacama Desert, South America.

WATERSPOUTS AND WATER DEVILS

Racing Water

These are watery versions of the violent storms that race over the land. Waterspouts form over the sea like a tornado, sucking up water. Water devils form over lakes.

Fact File WATERSPOUT FACTS...

* The tallest recorded waterspout was off the coast of Australia's New South Wales in 1898 at 5,000 feet tall.
* Usually less than 330 feet in diameter.
* Usually form in the fall when seas are warm.
* Waterspouts can pick up fish, frogs, and other objects to drop them far away.
* A waterspout in Spain killed six people when they were swept off a pier.

DiscoveryFact™

Water devils can kick up spray at the surface and probably caused a stir at Loch Ness, Scotland, when seen by monster hunters. Especially since the water near the surface makes bubbling noises and hissing and a long, necklike funnel rears up!

Did you know?

In 1879, three waterspouts hit the Tay Bridge in Scotland, which was already weakened by gales. A large section of bridge collapsed just as a train was crossing. The train plunged into the water, killing 75 people.

A waterspout forming near Elba, Italy.

STORM FORCE QUIZ

Can you unravel the scrambled-up storms below?

1. CHAIRRUNE

2. NOCYCLE

3. STIRWET

4. DONOART

5. TOWERSATUP

6. HOTPONY

7. STUDLIVED

Answers on page 96!

WILD WEATHER

Thunder and Lightning

The clouds that carry thunderstorms are called cumulonimbus clouds. Huge amounts of energy are released as ice crystals form in the top of the column of clouds. Water droplets and ice crystals bump into one another, storing up static electricity. This is how a storm begins.

DiscoveryFact™

Q: Which comes first—thunder or lightning?

A: They happen at the same instant, but light travels faster than sound, so you see the flash before you hear the roll of thunder.

Did you know?

Park Ranger Roy Sullivan of Virginia was struck by lightning seven times between 1942 and 1977. He had burns to his legs, chest, shoulder, and stomach, lost a toe nail, had his eyebrows burned off, and his hair caught fire twice.

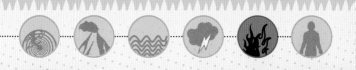

Discovery Rating
Danger factor: 2/10

Lightning over the plains of New Mexico.

Fact File STORMY STATS...

* A flash of lightning is a streak of electricity that travels between cloud and ground at up to 80,000 miles per second.
* Lightning zips through the sky, heating the air to 60,000°F. That's five times hotter than the surface of the sun.
* The hot air expands so quickly that it booms and cracks, creating thunder.
* Every day almost 45,000 thunderstorms happen—that's 2,000 right now!
* 100 flashes of lightning hit the Earth every second.

WILDFIRE

Hot Stuff

Bush and forest fires that start to burn out of control are sometimes caused by lightning strikes, especially in very dry weather. Fires are often caused by people, too, either carelessly—a campfire left burning, a cigarette tossed from a car—or, worse still, deliberately.

Fact File

MAJOR WILDFIRES...

* **Peshtigo, Wisconsin, 1871:** 1,500 people killed.
* **Oakland, California, 1991:** Huge areas of forest were burned and houses destroyed.
* **Peloponnese, Greece, 2007:** Fires raged for days and killed 64 people.
* **Victoria, Australia, 2009:** The worst fires in living memory killed over 200 people and destroyed vast amounts of property.

Did you know?
Fires can be good for forests, clearing deadwood and helping some seeds to germinate.

Firefighters battle the flames of a bushfire near Sydney, Australia, in 2007.

DiscoveryFact™

- On the ground, teams of firefighters dig trenches to create firebreaks.
- In the air, planes spray chemicals on the fires from above to help put out the flames.
- Surveillance planes fly over likely areas to spot fire outbreaks at an early stage.

GIANT HAILSTORMS

Ice Crystals

Hailstorms are born in thunderclouds when ice crystals are tossed up and down. Each time they go up and down, they get a new layer of ice.

Discovery Rating

Danger factor: 4/10

Hailstones from a hail storm in Leipzig, Germany, June, 2006.

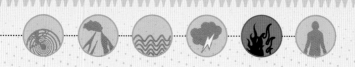

Fact File

HAIL SCALE...

TORRO (Tornado and Storm Research Organisation) created a scale to measure hailstones:

SIZE	SCALE	DIAMETER IN MM
0	pea	5-9
1	mothball	10-15
2	marble/grape	16-20
3	walnut	21-30
4	pigeon's egg/squash ball	31-40
5	golf ball/pullet's egg	41-50
6	hen's egg	51-60
7	tennis ball/cricket ball	61-75
8	large orange	76-90
9	grapefruit	91-100
10	melon	100+

Did you know?

The biggest storms only last about 10 minutes, but they can shatter windscreens, flatten crops and smash roofs.

DiscoveryFact™

In 1930, a small turtle disguised as a hailstone fell from the sky encased in ice.

ICE STORMS AND BLIZZARDS

Snow Trouble

Cold weather can be just as dangerous as wild storms. A blizzard is a storm with gale force winds of 35 mph or more, blowing snow, and with temperatures below 19°F. In a blizzard, it can be impossible to see anything through the "white-out" of whirling snow.

Discovery Rating

Danger factor: 7/10

Residents walk against heavy winds during a snowstorm in eastern China, 2005.

Fact File — MAJOR BLIZZARDS...

WHEN AND WHERE: 1888, north-eastern U.S.
DESCRIPTION: Began as rainstorm. 50 inches of snow fell. 400 people died.

WHEN AND WHERE: 1940, Great Britain
DESCRIPTION: A terrible freezing winter, probably the worst for 100 years.

WHEN AND WHERE: 1993, east coast of U.S.
DESCRIPTION: Known as "The White Hurricane." Lasted 3 days. Millions were without electricity. 200 people died.

WHEN AND WHERE: 2001, north China
DESCRIPTION: Lasted 3 days. 24 inches of snow mixed with sand from the Gobi Desert fell. 1,640,000 people were affected. 200,000 livestock were killed.

Did you know?

Freak ice storms happen when rain or melting snow suddenly freezes. Trees and plants are glazed with ice. It looks very beautiful, but can be dangerous. The electrical power lines sag under the weight of ice and can snap. Sometimes electrical towers collapse, too.

DiscoveryFact™

Strong winds make it even colder. A temperature of 25°F plus a wind blowing at 20 mph reduces the temperature to a bone-chilling −4°F.

AVALANCHE!

Scary Snowfall

As many as one million avalanches happen every year, with snow falling at up to 185 mph. They are caused by melting snow, by animals or skiers, sometimes by machinery, and occasionally by earthquakes.

Discovery Rating

Danger factor: 7/10

An avalanche in the Swiss Alps, 1999.

Fact File

MAJOR AVALANCHES...

WHEN AND WHERE: 1910, Washington State
DESCRIPTION: Spring avalanche pushed two trains and station house over 165-foot cliff.

WHEN AND WHERE: 1915-18, European Alps
DESCRIPTION: Avalanche caused by gunfire of soldiers fighting.

WHEN AND WHERE: 1950-51, Winter of Terror, Alps
DESCRIPTION: 649 major avalanches occurred, killing 265 people.

WHEN AND WHERE: 1962, Peru
DESCRIPTION: 3,000 deaths.

WHEN AND WHERE: 1970, Peru
DESCRIPTION: Earthquake triggered an avalanche. Caused a wave of snow, rock, soil, and water to travel 9 miles to the town of Yungay. Only 2,000 of the 25,000 inhabitants survived.

Did you know?

Rescue dogs can find victims buried in snow up to 13 feet deep and sometimes up to 33 feet deep. Only half of victims survive more than 30 minutes.

Eyewitness:

A survivor of the Yungay avalanche said, "I heard a deep muffled thunk as it fractured. Then it was like someone pulled the rug out from under me."

FLOODS

Water, Water, Everywhere!

Floods kill more people than all other natural disasters put together. They may be caused by torrential rains, by storm surges triggered by hurricanes, or by tsunamis.

Fact File MAJOR FLOODS...

1993	Mississippi River floods
1993	Floods in Japan caused by a tsunami
2004	Major flood in Boscastle, Great Britain
2005	Floods devastate Mumbai, India

YANGTZE RIVER, CHINA

1887	2 million people perish in floods
1931	Between 1 and 3.7 million die in floods on the huge plains
1938	Over 1 million die

BANGLADESH

1970	2 million killed
1998	Many millions homeless
2004	Bangladesh and India suffer terrible floods after the monsoon rains

Damage caused by freak floods in Boscastle, Great Britain, in 2004.

Discovery Rating

Danger factor: 10/10

Did you know?

Over half of the world's population lives near or on a coast.

DiscoveryFact™

El Niño is a warm current off the coast of South America affecting the climate of the whole continent. Every 5 to 7 years it heads towards the land, bringing heavy rains and flooding.

DROUGHTS

Dry and Deadly

Most disasters happen very suddenly and last for a few days at most. Droughts last for years and cause long-term problems.

Discovery Rating

Danger factor: 9/10

Fact File
DROUGHT INFO...

* One third of the world has less than 10 inches of rain per year. People will starve if rains fail.
* The Sahel in Africa has suffered long-term drought for over 30 years. Between 1968 and 1973, 250,000 people and 3.5 million cattle died.
* The Atacama Desert in Chile has not had rain for 400 years.

Did you know?
Low rainfall causes:
• Famine
• Poverty
• Illness through lack of proper food
• Danger of fire

DiscoveryFact™

Southeast Asia suffered a terrible drought in 1997-98. Fires raged for months and there were no monsoon rains to put them out.

Dry, cracked earth in the Atacama Desert, Chile.

DISEASES AND PANDEMICS

Coughs and sneezes...

Infectious diseases are a bigger threat than natural disasters. They cause millions of deaths each year.

A flu outbreak in 1918 killed 25–50 million people.

Fact File

SPREADING DISEASES...

* Viruses and bacteria are often carried by animals and insects and spread from one person to another.
* Viruses cause diseases like chickenpox, measles, and polio.
* Bacteria cause diseases like cholera.

Pandemic

A pandemic is a disease that spreads worldwide. "The Plague," or "Black Death" of medieval times, was a deadly pandemic. It was caused by the fleas on rats.

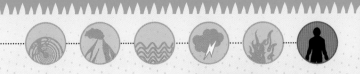

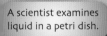

A scientist examines liquid in a petri dish.

Did you know?

The world's deadliest disease is malaria, spread by mosquitoes. Mosquitoes can also pass on diseases like yellow fever and dengue, a kind of fever-like flu.

PROTECTING OURSELVES

Super Science

We will never be able to control the forces of nature such as hurricanes and volcanoes, but scientists can continue to study them so that we understand more about how and why they happen.

Fact File STAYING SAFE...

Here are some of the ways in which we can protect ourselves:

WATER PRESERVATION—protection against drought, providing irrigation for crops.

VACCINATION—to protect ourselves against disease.

CLEAN WATER SUPPLY—especially in poor countries.

CLIMATE CONTROL—understanding how rising sea temperatures affect our planet and its weather systems.

INDEX

ANSWERS

Pages 22-23
1. d) tectonic plates
2. b) the epicenter
3. c) rotten eggs
4. b) your fingernails grow
5. a) Tokyo

Pages 40-41
1. False 2. True 3. True 4. False
5. True 6. False 7. False 8. True
9. False 10. False

Pages 62-63
1. c) The eye
2. b) Clockwise
3. d) In the Indian Ocean
4. b) The wall
5. a) Katrina

Pages 74-75
1. Hurricane
2. Cyclone
3. Twister
4. Tornado
5. Waterspout
6. Typhoon
7. Dust devil

CREDITS

Cover AFP/Getty Images, 8-9 AFP/Getty Images, 10-11 Time Inc./Time Life Pictures/Getty Images, 12-13 Code Red/Getty, 14-15 AFP/Getty Images, 16-17 AFP/Getty Images, 18-19 Uyen Le/Getty Images, 20-21 National Geographic/Getty Images, 22-23 AFP/Getty Images, 24-25 David Trood/Getty, 26-27 Philippe Bourseiller/Getty Images, 28-29 InterNetwork Media/Getty, 30-31 Frank Krahmer/Getty, 32-33 O.Louis Mazzatenta/Getty, 34-35 Philippe Bourseiller/Getty, 36-37 AFP/Getty Images, 38-39 National Geographic/Getty Images, 42-43 Panoramic Images/Getty, 44-45 Ian Waldie/Getty Images, 46-47 Getty Images News/Getty, 48-49 PORNCHAI KITTIWONGSAKUL/AFP/Getty Images, 50-51 World Perspectives/Getty, 52-53 StockTrek/Getty, 54-55 Kevin Horan/Getty, 56-57 AFP/Getty Images, 58-59 Christopher Pillitz/Getty Images, 60-61 David J. Phillip-Pool/Getty Images, 62 World Perspectives/Getty, 63 StockTrek/Getty, 64-65 Philippe Bourseiller/The Image Bank/Getty, 66-67 Alan R Moller/Getty Images, 68-69 Carsten Peter/National Geographic/Getty Images, Joel Sartore/Getty, 72-73 DEA/C.ANDREOLI/Getty, 74 left AFP/Getty Images, 74 right Kevin Horan/Getty, 75 top DEA/C.ANDREOLI/Getty, 75 bottom right Joel Sartore/Getty, 75 bottom left Philippe Bourseiller/The Image Bank/Getty, 76-77 Bruce Dale/National Geographic/Getty Images, 78-79 Getty Images News/Getty, 80-81 Getty Images News/Getty, 82-83 China Photos/Getty Images, 84-85 AFP/Getty Images, 86-87 Getty Images News/Getty, 88-89 Stuart McCall/Getty Images, 90-91 Lester Lefkowitz/Getty Images, 93 top Miguel Salmeron/Getty Images, 93 top right Joe Raedle/Getty Images, 93 bottom left Christopher Pillitz/Getty Images, 93 bottom Kim Heacox/Getty Images